Explorers of Canada

David Thompson

By Ellen Rodger

Explorers of Canada is published by Beech Street Books
27 Stewart Rd. Collingwood, ON Canada L9Y 4M7

www.beechstreetbooks.ca

Produced by Calcium Creative Ltd

Cover illustration by Damian Zain

Photographs ©: Archives of Ontario: p. 27l; Flickr: Jasperdo-John Schrantz: p. 5; Libraries and Archives Canada: Canada Dep., of Interior/Library and Archives Canada/PA-044545/a044545: p. 21b; Library and Archives Canada, Acc. No. 1972-26-1406: p. 13t; Library and Archives Canada, Acc. No. 1972-26-9: p. 25t; Library and Archives Canada, Acc. No. 1989-401-3/e011154434: p. 23; Library and Archives Canada, Acc. No. 1994-254-1.40R Acquire with the assistance of Hoechst and Celanese Canada and with a grant from the Department of the Canadian Heritage under the Cultural Property Export and Import Act: p. 20; Library and Archives Canada, Acc. No. 1996-475-2: p. 8b; Library and Archives Canada, PA-051909: p. 26; Library and Archives Canada, PA-169585: p. 17t; National Park Service: p. 16; Harry Palmer: p. 21t; Shutterstock: Jody Ann: p. 7; Autumn Sky Photography: p. 4; Robert Bohrer: p. 22; CherylRamalho: p. 6t; EB Adventure Photography: p. 9; Everett Historical: p. 11b; Kavram: pp. 3r, 17b; Tatsuo Nakamura: p. 29b; Vaclav Sebek: pp. 3b, 8t; Shots by Daniel: p. 15t; Wikimedia Commons: p. 6b; Karl Bodmer: pp. 18-19t, 19b; Canada Post: p. 29t; Canadian Press Syndicate: p. 27r; Edward S. Curtis: pp. 1, 11t; Jason Hollinger: p. 10; Jonathunder: p. 15b; Own work: p. 28; Panda~thwiki: p. 13b; David Thompson: p. 25b

Editors: Kelly Spence, Sarah Eason, and Harriet McGregor

Designers: Jeni Child, Clare Webber, and Paul Myerscough

Proofreader and Indexer: Wendy Scavuzzo

Photo Researcher: Rachel Blount

Library and Archives Canada Cataloguing in Publication

Title: David Thompson / by Ellen Rodger.
Names: Rodger, Ellen, author.
Description: Series statement: Explorers of Canada | Includes bibliographical references and index.
Identifiers: Canadiana (print) 20190122749 | Canadiana (ebook) 20190122854 | ISBN 9781773085876 (hardcover) | ISBN 9781773086262 (softcover) | ISBN 9781773086651 (PDF) | ISBN 9781773087047 (HTML)
Subjects: LCSH: Thompson, David, 1770-1857—Juvenile literature. | LCSH: Explorers—Canada—Biography—Juvenile literature. | LCSH: Cartographers—Canada—Biography—Juvenile literature. | LCSH: Fur traders—Canada—Biography—Juvenile literature. | LCSH: Northwest, Canadian—Discovery and exploration—Juvenile literature. | LCGFT: Biographies.
Classification: LCC FC3212.1.T46 R63 2019 | DDC 971.03/092—dc23

Printed in the United States of America
Mankato, MN
August 2019

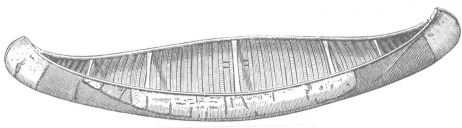

Contents

Who Was David Thompson?

David Thompson has been called the greatest land geographer who ever lived. From 1784 to 1815, he was a **trader**, explorer, and mapmaker for two of the biggest **fur trading** companies in North America. He travelled and **surveyed** thousands of kilometres of wilderness on foot, snowshoe, dog-sled, horseback, and by canoe.

Thompson was born in Westminster, England. He was the first child of Ann and David Thompson. The family lived comfortably until 1772, when Thompson's father died. Without much money, Ann moved the family to a poorer area of the city. In 1777, Thompson was sent to Grey Coat Hospital, which was a **charity school** for poor children.

May 20 1784

Thompson begins working for the Hudson's Bay Company (HBC).

April 29 1777

Thompson starts school.

April 30 1770

David Thompson is born in Westminster, England.

Thompson first attempted to cross the Rocky Mountains in 1801. He failed, but later tried again.

At Grey Coat Hospital, Thompson received a good education. Thompson learned mathematics, **navigation**, geography, and mapmaking, as well as how to read and write. In 1784, after finishing school at age 14, he became an **apprentice** with the Hudson's Bay Company (HBC). That spring, he set sail on board the *Prince Rupert*, bound for North America.

This statue of David Thompson shows him holding a navigation tool called a sextant.

THE HUDSON'S BAY COMPANY

The HBC was established in 1670. It began when King Charles II of England gave French fur traders Pierre-Esprit Radisson and Médard Chouart des Groseilliers a **Royal Charter**. This charter gave them sole control over the fur trade in an area of land and water that drained into Hudson Bay. It was known as Rupert's Land. It covered 3.9 million square kilometres. There were dozens of forts and **trading posts** throughout the territory. The HBC employed men as traders, boatmen, clerks, and navigators. The men worked at the forts, explored the area, and expanded the HBC's fur trade business. Many of these men, like David Thompson, came from Great Britain.

Fort Churchill

Hudson Bay

York Factory

RUPERT'S LAND

Montréal

Working for the Company

In September 1784, Thompson arrived by ship at Fort Churchill, on the southwest shore of Hudson Bay, in what is now Manitoba. At the time, it was the HBC's most-northerly trading post. The HBC had a near **monopoly** on the fur trade, with hundreds of posts positioned in an area that covered thousands of kilometres.

Trading posts were often called "factories" because they were under the authority of a factor, or **merchant** trader, who was in charge of buying and selling furs. While out travelling and exploring, traders stopped at factories to rest, spend the winter, or pick up and drop off supplies. Resting at the trading posts was a welcome relief after months in the wilderness.

The landscape at Fort Churchill is wild and windswept.

The HBC built several trading posts at the mouths of rivers along Hudson Bay.

David Thompson's first years with "the company" were spent as a clerk at a number of trading posts. At Fort Churchill, one of his jobs was to inventory, or count, supplies. Another duty was to copy the papers of the fort's **governor**, Samuel Hearne. Hearne had explored far into the northwest and Arctic for the HBC. Reading of his adventures likely fueled Thompson's desire to explore.

During the summer, traders returned to the post with their **pelts**. Beaver was the most common fur. During good years, more than 100,000 pelts were traded. As a clerk, Thompson helped record the transactions, or sales, between traders and **Indigenous** Peoples.

A European craze for hats made from beaver fur made the fur trade profitable. The hats were made from the beaver's undercoat and were waterproof.

September 1784

Thompson arrives at Fort Churchill.

MOSQUITOES

During his first summer in North America, Thompson wrote in his journals that "Summer such as it is, comes at once, and with it **myriads** of tormenting Musketoes." No one could escape the misery of the bug bites, whether outside or inside the trading post. Thompson noted that the local Indigenous Peoples rubbed their bodies with oil made from sturgeon fish to soothe the itch.

Living Off the Land

During his first years in North America, Thompson recorded information about the wildlife and Indigenous Peoples near the factories. He noted the fierce polar bears near Fort Churchill, and wrote about how the Indigenous Peoples lived off the land. His admiration for their hunting skills was clear.

In fall 1785, Thompson got his first taste of adventure. He was sent to York Factory, about 241 kilometres to the south. He travelled with two Indigenous men who were hired to deliver mail between trading posts. On the expedition, they lived off the land. They slept on the ground and ate whatever they could hunt. When they arrived at York Factory, Thompson's guides were rewarded with brandy and tobacco.

Polar bears gathered on the shore near Fort Churchill each fall. They waited for Hudson Bay to freeze so they could head out and hunt for seals.

Thompson travels to York Factory.

1785

York Factory was isolated and served as a fur trading post for 273 years.

That winter, Thompson was part of a hunting party that supplied York Factory with fresh meat, such as fish, rabbit, grouse, marten, and fox. During the next two years, Thompson travelled between trading posts. He was one of the traders who helped set up Manchester House, the most remote HBC post at the time. During that time, he learned to speak Cree. At the same time, other fur traders were building forts in the area. The HBC was eager to expand its network of trading posts to the west.

Winter 1785

Thompson hunts to supply meat to York Factory.

July 21 1786

He heads out with a team to set up more forts along the Saskatchewan River.

August 1786

Thompson helps establish Manchester House.

FLASH >>> FORWARD

Changed Land

Much of the wilderness Thompson surveyed still exists and some of it is almost untouched. But large parts of the landscape were settled by Europeans throughout the 1900s. Where plains existed, there are now farms and cities. Borders between Canada and the United States are now set. Some rivers have been forever altered, and the Rocky Mountains are now tourist destinations.

Modern explorers can take the highway through the Rocky Mountain territory that David Thompson travelled on foot, horseback, and by canoe.

9

Winter Among the Piikani

Fur traders relied on **alliances** with Indigenous Peoples. Different Indigenous nations worked as trappers and guides. They shared their knowledge of the land and its vast network of rivers and lakes with Europeans traders. These relationships had a lasting impact on Indigenous Peoples. The arrival of Europeans also brought new diseases that killed thousands of Indigenous Peoples living on the plains. Trade put weapons such as guns in the hands of warriors, which increased warfare between Indigenous nations.

1787 -88

Thompson spends a winter among the Piikani.

Spruce trees and lodge pole pines grow near grassy and swampy areas of the foothills, in what is now Alberta. In the 1700s, this was rich fur trading land.

The Piikani are people of the Great Plains. Their territory once included large parts of modern Alberta and Montana.

When he was just 17 years old, Thompson and six other men were sent to gain the friendship and business of the Piikani, who were camped in the foothills of the Rocky Mountains. His journals record information about how the Piikani lived. During the winter months, Thompson stayed with an **elder** named Saukamappee who helped him learn the Blackfoot language spoken by the Piikani. Saukamappee also told him stories, including one about how **smallpox** killed many of his people. They caught the deadly disease after a party of Piikani came upon the camp of another Indigenous community and one man stole a blanket of another man who had died from smallpox. That man also became ill and infected 20 others, who were all separated to prevent more deaths.

SMALLPOX

Smallpox is an infectious disease that spreads easily from one person to another. People who catch the disease develop small pus-filled blisters. When Europeans arrived in North America, they brought the disease with them. It killed many Indigenous Peoples, who had no **immunity** to it. More than 200 years later, in 1980, the disease was declared **eradicated** by the World Health Organization (WHO).

This man is infected with smallpox. This disease killed thousands of Piikani people during an outbreak in 1837.

Injuries and Setbacks

In fall 1788, Thompson was stationed at Manchester House. In December, Thompson fell while out hunting. He broke his right leg and was carried back to Manchester House. In spring 1789, Thompson was taken to Cumberland House. That fall, Philip Turnor, the HBC's chief surveyor, arrived. Turnor tutored Thompson in math, surveying, and **astronomy**. Turnor was impressed with his student. Thompson took notes and measurements three or four times a day. It was later confirmed that his measurements of the location of Cumberland House were near perfect. At that time, Thompson lost the sight in his right eye. Thompson's poor eyesight and leg injury prevented Turnor from taking him along that summer as he explored westward to Athabasca country. Thompson returned to York Factory to finish his apprenticeship.

December 23
1788

Thompson breaks his leg near Manchester House.

Winter 1789-90

Thompson learns astronomy from Turnor at Cumberland House.

Summer 1790

Thompson is sent to York Factory. He surveys along the way.

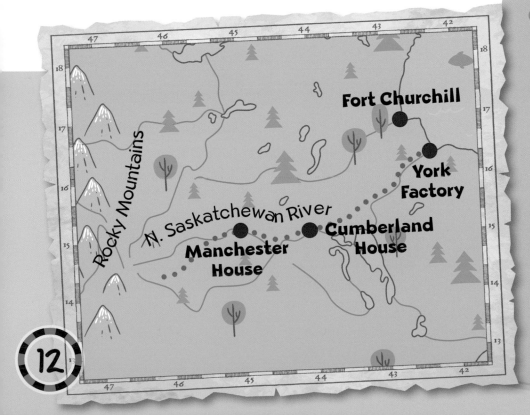

Thompson was careful with his navigation equipment. It allowed him to take accurate measurements from which he made his maps.

FROM SERVICE TO SURVEYOR

In 1790, Thompson completed his seven-year apprenticeship. He was entitled to the "suit of clothes" given to all HBC apprentices. But instead, Thompson asked for a set of surveying tools. This included a sextant, an artificial horizon, and nautical almanacs. A sextant is used to measure the angle between the **horizon** and a **celestial** body, such as the sun or a star. An artificial horizon is a tool that creates an artificial, or fake, horizon in a small container of **mercury**. Nautical almanacs are books that describe the position of celestial objects. Thompson was determined to improve his skills and be appointed as a surveyor—a position that would allow him to explore more. The HBC provided him with these tools, plus a new suit of clothes.

Thompson returns to Cumberland House.

Winter 1790

Early explorers used the position of certain stars in the sky to navigate. They helped explorers figure out a geographic position on Earth.

13

Master to the Northward

By 1792, with his apprenticeship complete, Thompson was eager to prove his value to the company. To the southwest of York Factory, between the Nelson and Churchill Rivers, lay what Thompson called "Muskrat Country." Thompson was sent there to find a shorter route to Athabasca country by way of Reindeer Lake—the area surveyed by Turnor a few years earlier. There was increasing competition from other fur traders, so the HBC wanted to expand trading there. For five years, Thompson travelled, surveyed, and mapped rivers and lakes in what is now northeast and northwest Saskatchewan. But he did not discover a better route to Athabasca country.

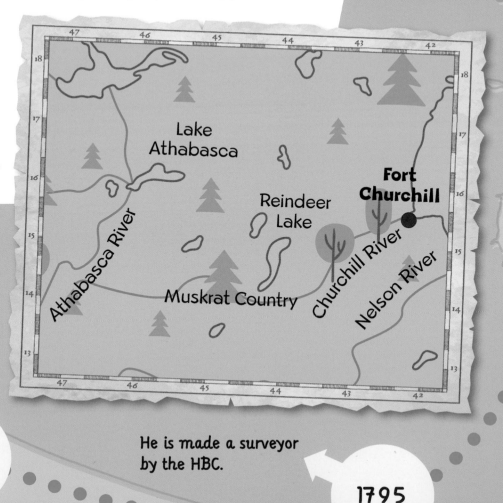

Lake Athabasca

Reindeer Lake

Fort Churchill

Athabasca River

Muskrat Country

Churchill River

Nelson River

Thompson begins to trade and survey in the Athabasca region.

1792

He is made a surveyor by the HBC.

1795

Thompson was frustrated by his progress exploring the Athabasca region. He felt it was slowed by the HBC's focus on trade.

In spring 1795, Thompson learned that he had been made a surveyor by the HBC. A year later, he was named "Master to the Northward." This new role would give him greater responsibility in the fur trade. But this did not interest Thompson, although it meant more money. The ambitious young explorer wanted to spend his time surveying rather than trading pelts.

NORTH WEST COMPANY

The North West Company (NWC) was a fur trading company set up in 1779 by a group of Montréal merchants. It quickly became the HBC's biggest competitor. Known as the Nor'Westers, the employees of the NWC knew their geography and had dozens of trading posts spread throughout the west. Unlike the HBC, the Nor'Westers spent the winter west of Hudson Bay. But the HBC had a faster route to supply furs to Europe from Fort Churchill, on Hudson Bay. The NWC sent its furs through Montréal, which took much longer.

This building is a reconstructed NWC trading post on Snake River in what is now Minnesota.

Joining the Competition

Thompson was becoming frustrated working for the HBC. So in 1797, Thompson did something unexpected. He walked 120 kilometres east to Grand Portage (in present-day Minnesota) and joined the HBC's biggest competitor, the NWC.

The NWC's partners and traders met each summer at Grand Portage, a depot on Lake Superior.

The NWC welcomed him. But the HBC was upset. It was common for traders to give one year's notice that they were leaving the company. Many people were angry at Thompson. But at the NWC, he was encouraged to survey the land. On foot, by canoe, on horseback, and by dogsled, from his first days with the NWC, Thompson was constantly on the move. He set out to survey, sketch, and map rivers, lakes, and land in the west.

Thompson leaves HBC.

May 1797

July 1797

Thompson joins the NWC.

CANOES

The canoes used by traders were based on the birchbark canoes of the Indigenous Peoples. **Brigades** of the *canot du maître*, or Montréal canoe, paddled by **voyageurs**, were used to bring furs across larger bodies of water. NWC traders brought furs to Lachine, Québec, from Grand Portage, and later from Fort William (Ontario) on Lake Superior. From Montréal, the valuable furs were sent on to Europe.

At first, the NWC and HBC both used canoes to travel. After 1821, the HBC used larger scows, a type of large flat-bottomed boat such as this one.

In the spring and summer, a team of men travelled in *canota du nord* (canoes of the north). These smaller canoes were suited for paddling northern lakes and rivers. They were also light enough to portage, or carry, between bodies of water. Travelling by canoe was dangerous. Rapids, rocks, and shallow rivers could easily flip or damage a canoe. Drowning was also common.

Traders navigated wild rivers by portaging their canoes around areas with falls, such as these on the Athabasca River.

The 49th Parallel

In 1783, the United States gained independence from Britain. In 1794, Britain and the United States signed a **treaty** to establish the boundary between the United States and Canada, which was still a British **colony**. British trading posts in U.S. territory needed to be relocated. This treaty is known as Jay's Treaty.

In July 1797, Thompson and a crew were given the task of mapping NWC trading posts along the new border, which was known as the 49th parallel. The NWC provided Thompson with everything he desired for the expedition, including tobacco, ammunition, and small items to trade with the Indigenous Peoples.

Thompson spends time with the Mandan and Hidatsa peoples.

Winter 1797

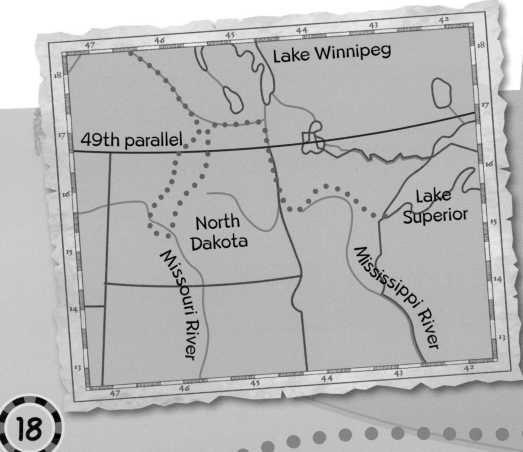

Lake Winnipeg

49th parallel

North Dakota

Missouri River

Lake Superior

Mississippi River

THE MANDAN AND HIDATSA

While charting NWC trading posts, the crew travelled south into what is now North Dakota. There, Thompson visited the Mandan and Hidatsa, Indigenous farmers who were known for trading corn. Thompson spent a month there, trying to convince the farmers to travel to NWC posts to trade. During his time with the Mandan, Thompson made a dictionary of 375 Mandan words. He also noted how they pounded dry corn into meal, which they mixed with water into a paste that was then cooked.

This painting shows the inside of Mandan housing in the 1800s. The people are gathered around a fire pit.

It was a difficult journey and when winter came, the party travelled by dogsled. They camped in tents that offered little protection from the weather. They were also on the lookout for the Sioux, an Indigenous community now made up of the Dakota, Lakota, and Nakota, who were enemies of the Mandan. In ten months, Thompson covered a huge territory and also discovered one of the headwaters of the Mississippi River at Turtle Lake.

The Mandan used dogsleds for travel during the winter.

A Country Marriage

While travelling back to Grand Portage in 1799, Thompson stopped at Île-à-la-Crosse, a trading post in what is now north-central Saskatchewan. There, he married 13-year-old Charlotte Small, the daughter of NWC partner Patrick Small. Charlotte's mother was Cree and, like her daughter after her, was a country wife.

At the time, fur traders often married local women when working in the bush. These women were called country wives. Marriages to country wives helped the traders establish good relationships with Indigenous communities. They later abandoned their Indigenous wives when they returned home, also abandoning any children they had with them at the same time. Charlotte's father had done this. For these men, the marriage was only beneficial while they were in the wilderness.

Spring 1799

1798

David Thompson spends the winter on Lac la Biche and builds a trading post.

He follows the Athabasca River to Clearwater River.

Both the HBC and the NWC had forts at Île-à-la-Crosse.

But Thompson and Charlotte's marriage was unusual—it was a permanent partnership. Charlotte accompanied Thompson on many of his treks and proved a valuable team member. Her skills were useful in the wilderness. For example, Charlotte would have known how to make pemmican. This Indigenous staple was an important food source for fur traders. To make pemmican, meat was dried, and then pounded into a powder. The powder was mixed with berries and animal fat, and cooled. Pemmican was easy to transport and a good source of energy, particularly during the winter when food was scarce.

This statue celebrates Thompson and Charlotte's partnership. Her language skills and knowledge of how to live on the land helped them survive while exploring.

June 10 1799 → He marries Charlotte Small at Île-à-la-Crosse.

FLASH >>> FORWARD

The Métis

The children of European traders and Indigenous women became known as the Métis. Over time, they developed their own unique culture and their own language, called Michif. Today, the Métis are recognized as one of three Indigenous communities in Canada.

A woman and her three children are pictured here at Île-à-la-Crosse, a mostly Métis community.

Across the Mountains

With increasing competition from the HBC, the NWC was determined to extend its trade west of the Rocky Mountains. Thompson made three attempts to cross the Rocky Mountains in expeditions from 1800 to 1801, but failed to find a **pass**. He finally made it on June 25, 1807. His party included Charlotte and three of their children. They came through a pass used by generations of Ktunaxa and Piikani people. It was later called Howse Pass. To increase trade for the NWC, Thompson and his men built several trading posts on both sides of the mountains. He spent years surveying more land and extending the NWC trade to the Ktunaxa and Interior Salish people.

1800 -01

Thompson works as a trader in what is now Alberta but explores into the Rocky Mountains.

1804

Thompson becomes an NWC partner.

Howse Pass was named for HBC factor Joseph Howse. He travelled through the pass two years after Thompson.

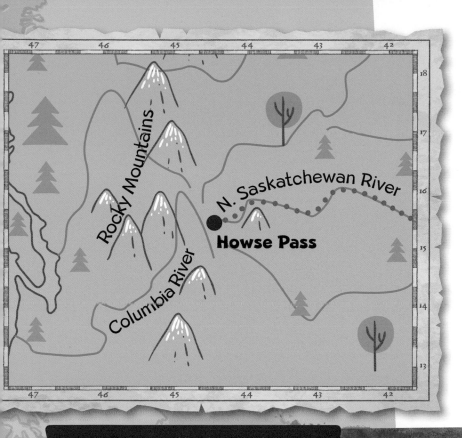

Thompson gained great respect for the Indigenous Peoples that he met during his expedition. He felt uncomfortable with the NWC trading style, which often included trading alcohol with Indigenous trappers in exchange for fur. Alcohol was cheap, which meant the fur trade companies spent less to get their furs. Thompson also disliked how people behaved when they were drunk. He often smashed barrels of alcohol the NWC provided him with.

Voyageurs camped by the river during their journeys along it by canoe. Their canoes carried trade goods to the northwest. They carried furs back to Montréal.

WINTERING PARTNER

In July 1804, Thompson was promoted to NWC wintering partner, and given two **shares** of the company. Wintering partners were men who had proved their worth in the bush, spending their winters in the northwest gathering furs or surveying. They were rewarded with a small share in the company—and more trading responsibility. The NWC's Montréal agents and owners owned the majority of the company and determined how things should run. As fur trading was hard work most suitable for the young and strong, Thompson's small ownership share would allow him to eventually retire.

Journey Along the Columbia

By 1810, competition between the HBC and NWC had increased. Around the same time, the Pacific Fur Company (PFC) was pushing into the area west of the Rocky Mountains from the south. The PFC owner, American John Jacob Astor, wanted to set up a trading post at the mouth of the Columbia River. The NWC sent Thompson to the west to establish an overland route to the mouth of the Columbia, and set up trading partnerships with the Indigenous Peoples of the coast.

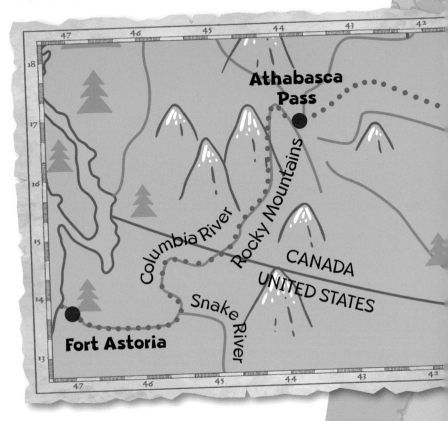

The expedition was difficult. In the mountains, Thompson's brigade encountered angry Piikani warriors. The Piikani were unhappy with the NWC for supplying weapons to their enemies, the Interior Salish. They wanted to block any further trade across the mountains. To avoid fighting, Thompson headed north to the Athabasca Pass. Freezing temperatures and deep snow forced the men to abandon their horses. Many **deserted** the expedition.

1807-10 — Thompson trades furs and surveys the territory of the Interior Salish and Ktunaxa peoples.

July 1811 — He establishes a new trading post at Snake River.

Thompson often travelled on snowshoes. The wide snowshoes prevented him from sinking into the snow.

At last, Thompson and his three remaining men made it across the mountains. They built a cedar canoe and followed the river. Along the way, the traders established relationships with new Indigenous trading partners. On July 15, Thompson arrived at Fort Astoria, where the PFC had already set up a trading post. Thompson spent a short time at the fort before heading back up the Columbia. His historic survey of the river would be his last major expedition.

FLASH >>> FORWARD

Great Map of the Northwest

In 1813 and 1814, Thompson created his great map of the Northwest. He glued together 25 sheets of paper to make the huge map. It showed the many lakes, rivers, and mountains he had surveyed. Thompson's "great map" of the North-West Territory of the Province of Canada hung at the NWC headquarters at Fort William.

Thompson's great map measures 2.13 metres high by 3.30 metres wide. A copy now hangs at the Archives of Ontario.

July 15 1811

He arrives at Fort Astoria.

Retirement and Death

The life of a fur trader was rough. While exploring through the Rocky Mountains, Thompson is believed to have remarked that he had hardly spent any time in a cabin in years. By 1812, he was 42 years old and had spent 28 years in the wilderness. Thompson decided to retire. He and his family headed east to Montréal.

In 1815, Thompson moved his family to a farm in Williamstown, Ontario. From 1817 to 1826, he worked as a surveyor marking the Canada–United States border from the St. Lawrence River to Lake of the Woods, a distance of about 1600 kilometres. In 1825, the NWC went **bankrupt** and Thompson lost his **pension**. He continued his work as a surveyor in Ontario and Québec, but a series of bad business decisions left Thompson poor. In 1846, Thompson started organizing his journals and writing an account of his travels through North America. He died in 1857 before he could publish his book. Charlotte died three months later. They were together for 58 years. Both were buried in Mount Royal Cemetery in Montréal.

1815

He moves to Williamstown, and buys a farm.

Upon retiring, Thompson purchased this home and land in Williamstown, Ontario. He later fell on hard times and had to sell it.

1812

Thompson retires and moves to Montréal with his family.

1814

He publishes his famous Map of the North-West Territory of the Province of Canada.

It is remarkable that Thompson's journals (above), found by Joseph Burr Tyrrell (right), survived in such great shape. Thompson had taken them with him wherever he travelled across Canada.

Thompson dies in Montréal.

February 10 1857

J. B. Tyrrell publishes Thompson's journals.

1916

FLASH >>> FORWARD

Journals Rediscovered

For almost 60 years, Thompson's accomplishments remained largely unrecognized. Then along came mapmaker and geologist, Joseph Burr Tyrrell. He was part of a group that mapped the Rocky Mountains for the Canadian government in the 1880s. The old maps he was given were highly accurate, but nobody knew who had made them. After some research, Tyrrell discovered the maps came from Thompson's early journals and field notes. He found and bought Thompson's manuscript and journals, then published them.

Thompson's Legacy

Unlike many early explorers, there are few books written about David Thompson. There are even fewer statues and monuments. Despite having explored and surveyed thousands of kilometres from Québec to British Columbia, and the Great Lakes to the Arctic **watershed**, he is lesser-known. His work, however, lives on in his maps and journals.

Thompson's detailed maps of the northwest were used as base maps by later geographers and explorers of Canada and the northwest United States. Thompson was a painstaking notetaker who kept 101 journals about his journeys into the wilderness. His journals were discovered and published well after his death. They give an early glimpse of a land untouched by European settlement. Thompson may have been unique among European explorers for his respect for Indigenous Peoples and their knowledge. His journals also provide lots of information about nature and animals.

This statue of Thompson and his guides is in Lac la Biche, Alberta. Thompson arrived there in 1798 while searching for trade routes.

Today, Thompson is recognized as one of Canada's most important mapmakers. In 1927, the Canadian government named him a National Historic Person. Important sites from his travels have been made National Historic Sites, including Howse Pass, Athabasca Pass, Kootenae House, Rocky Mountain House, and Boat Encampment. In 1957, Canada Post released a stamp honouring the 100-year anniversary of his death. Today, there is a highway in Alberta named for the explorer.

This stamp issued in 1957 shows Thompson surveying a landscape while dressed in Indigenous clothing.

FLASH >>> FORWARD

Exploration Continues

In 2018, Parks Canada announced that its new research boat would be called the RV *David Thompson*. The explorer's legacy of discovery will continue as the boat is used to explore the Pacific, Atlantic, and Arctic Oceans, as well as the Great Lakes.

The David Thompson Highway runs through Banff National Park in Alberta.

Glossary

alliances partnerships in which people agree to work together

apprentice person who learns a job by studying for a fixed time with someone skilled in that job

astronomy study of the sun, stars, and other space objects

bankrupt not having enough money to pay what is owed

brigades groups of people who are organized to work together

celestial relating to the sky or space

charity school school for poor children funded by donations

colony area controlled by a far-away country

deserted quit one's assignment or job

elder person respected because of their age, knowledge, and experience

eradicated completely destroyed

fur trading buying and selling of animal skins

governor leader of a large organization

horizon line where Earth and the sky seem to meet

immunity the ability to resist an infection

Indigenous native to a place

merchant a person who buys and sells large amounts of goods

mercury silver-white metal

monopoly complete control over a supply of goods

myriads great numbers of

navigation finding out how to get from one place to another

pass gap in a mountainous area

pelts animal skins

pension money paid by a company to a person who is no longer working for it

Royal Charter document issued by a king or queen that gives rights to a person or group

shares units of ownership in a company

smallpox disease that is easily spread and results in a skin rash; it can be deadly

surveyed measured and examined an area of land

trader person who buys and sells

trading posts buildings where trade took place

treaty formal agreement between two or more political groups, such as countries

voyageurs boatmen employed by trading companies to transport goods and people

watershed area drained by a river system

TO LEARN MORE

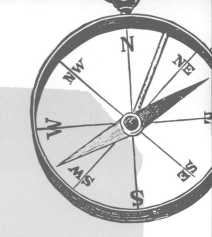

BOOKS

Andra-Warner, Elle. *Hudson's Bay Company Adventures: Tales of Canada's Fur Traders*. Victoria, BC: Heritage House Publishing, 2009.

Peterson, Cris. *Birchbark Brigade: A Fur Trade History*. Honesdale, PA: Calkins Creek, 2009.

Shardlow, Tom. *Mapping the Wilderness: The Story of David Thompson*. Toronto, ON: Napoleon and Company, 2006.

Smith, James K. *David Thompson*. Markham, ON: Fitzhenry & Whiteside, 2003.

WEBSITES

Discover more about David Thompson at the Archives of Ontario:
www.archives.gov.on.ca/en/explore/online/thompson/index.aspx

Learn more about David Thompson and the HBC at:
www.hbcheritage.ca/people/explorers/david-thompson

The Canadian Museum of History has a lot of information about David Thompson:
www.historymuseum.ca/cmc/exhibitions/hist/biography/biographi207e.html

Log on to The Canadian Encyclopedia to learn more:
www.thecanadianencyclopedia.ca/en/article/david-thompson

Index

ABOUT THE AUTHOR

Ellen Rodger has been a graveyard landscaper, newspaper reporter, and editor. She has picked blueberries near South Porcupine, Ontario, taken Cree lessons in Flin Flon, Manitoba, and once stuck her feet in glacial meltwater in Alberta. She has also written dozens of books. Like David Thompson, she was wonderstruck when she first saw the Rocky Mountains.